THE TEN COMMANDMENTS

Milo Kearney

Vivian Kearney

ISBN-10: 1-63065-090-0
ISBN-13: 978-1-63065-090-2

PUKIYARI PUBLISHERS
www.pukiyari.com

To our son Sean (who inspired this project), daughter-in-law Lisa, daughter Kathleen, and son-in-law Danny Anzak, who helped with computer work and suggestions, and to our grandsons Elijah, Benjamin, and Jeremy Anzak and Ian and Collin Kearney, in hopes that they will grow up to be mighty men of God.

TABLE OF CONTENTS

Short Version of the Ten Commandments
(Exodus 20:1-14)

1. I am the Lord thy God. Thou shalt have no other gods before me.

2. Thou shalt not make any graven images and bow down to them and serve them.

3. Thou shalt not take the name of the Lord Thy God in vain.

4. Remember the Sabbath day to keep it holy.

5. Honor thy father and thy mother.

6. Thou shalt not kill.

7. Thou shalt not commit adultery.

8. Thou shalt not steal.

9. Thou shalt not bear false witness.

10. Thou shalt not covet.

The Illustrations

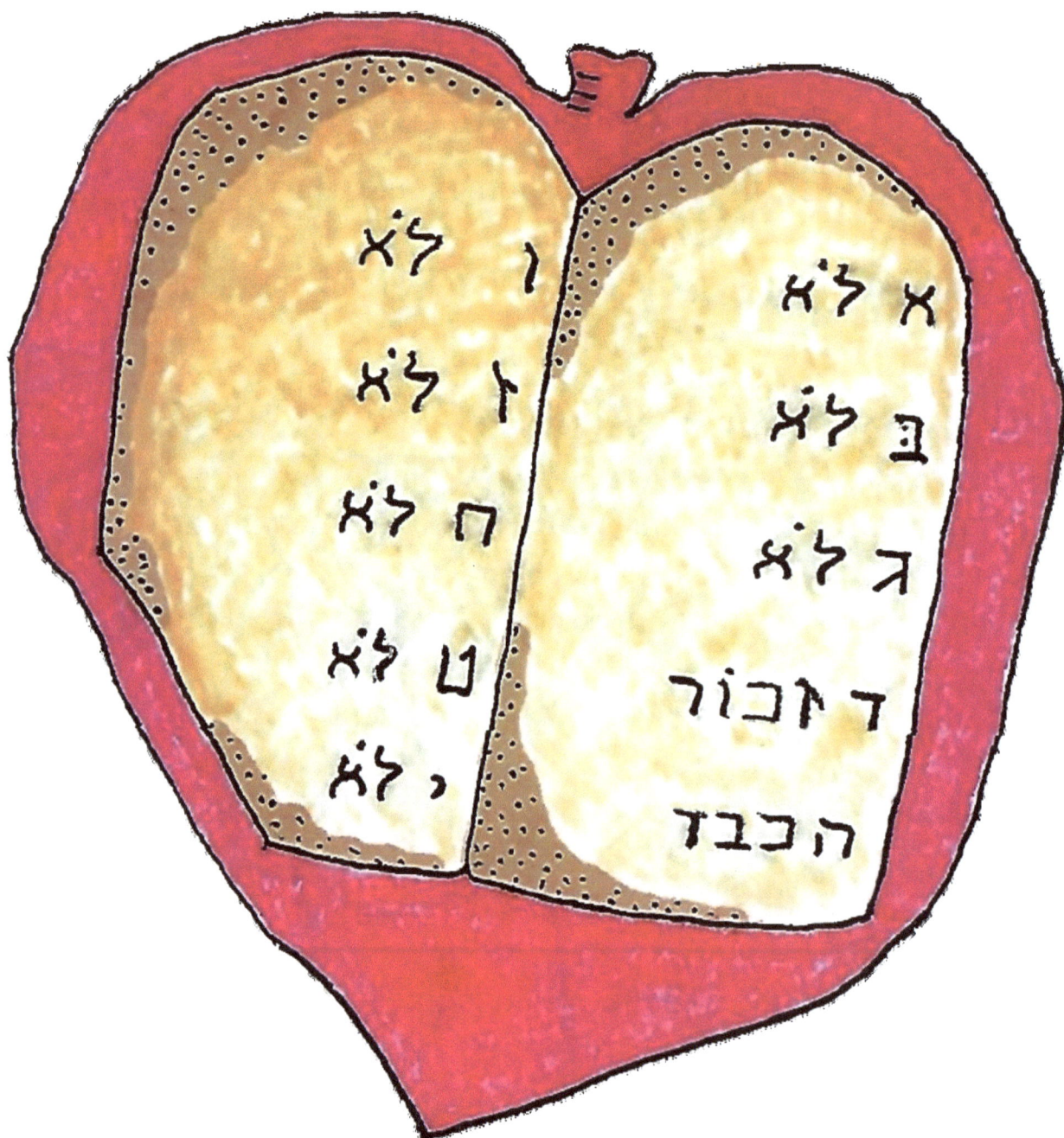

Introduction

God gave ten rules to guide our lives,
  for sons and daughters, husbands, wives.
And to keep us aware of these commands,
  He put ten fingers on our hands.

With His own great fingers shooting sparks,
  God burned these rules into our hearts.
Five rules towards Him direct our sight,
  Five rules call for our *menschlichkeit*.

Like two stone tablets in our chest,
  they tell us what is right and best.
Some people in the Bible show
  Just what God meant when He told us so.

Some obeyed, and they were blest.
  Others did as they thought best.

The First Commandment (Daniel 6)

We are warned in rule number one
  to worship God and Him alone.
The Bible tells about a man
  who obeyed this rule and fit God's plan.

His name was Daniel. He served the King,
  giving wise advice on everything.
His master, Darius, ruled the land
  of Persia with a mighty hand.

Darius' word was law, and, when he spoke,
  he had the ears of all his folk.
Darius liked Daniel, but, of late,
  he wondered about his loyalty to the State.

Daniel wasn't allowed to go over his head
  to appeal for help to his own God instead.
But Daniel knew that this would place
  false gods over God and king over faith.

Going to his room three times a day,
  beside an open window he would pray.
He placed his life into God's hand
  and didn't try to hide his stand.

The royal princes objected and blamed,
  calling for Daniel to be arrested and shamed.
They brought him to trial before some angry men
  and decided to throw him to lions in a den.

They dropped him down in while the lions did roar
  and by rolling a stone blocked the way through the door.
Then all through the night they left Daniel inside,
  and fully expected that Daniel had died.

But God is the Lord of the lions, you know,
  and he had them all sit very calm in a row.
Twelve nicer pussycats never were seen,
  and the night sped by quickly, as if 'twere a dream.

In the morning, the King came rushing to find
  what had happened to Daniel in all of that time.
He rolled off the stone that was blocking the door,
  and there Daniel was sitting, as well as before.

The King pulled Daniel out, shouting, "You're good as new!"
  Then he threw in the men who had said things untrue.
So Daniel was saved, honoring God, as is fit,
  while those who put men first now had to submit.

The Second Commandment (Exodus 32)

Some people ask, "Is it not good
  to worship a statue of our God?"
They mistake the echo for the song,
  and God has warned us it is wrong.

God's laws are holy, just, and pure.
  His punishment is strict and sure.
Those who push his patience to extremes
  learn what God says is what God means.

When God's people were in the wilderness,
  having fled from Egypt's sinfulness,
they waited by the mountainside
  while Moses climbed to seek God, his guide.

The people waited night and day.
  It seemed whole weeks had passed away.
They complained to Aaron, "Moses is dead."
  Let's honor God with a statue instead."

"Like a young and mighty bull is He,
  so let's show Him in this sort of majesty."
Aaron melted earrings on their behalf
  And shaped them into a golden calf.

They built an altar deep and wide
  and burned meat offerings at the side.
They sang and danced so merrily,
  and threw their clothes off in their glee.

Their ruckus sounded like a war.
  Moses fumed with rage, and God still more.
Moses raised the tablets with God's writs
  and smashed them into little bits.

Next Moses grabbed the golden calf
  and broke it fiercely into half.
Into powdered dust the gold was ground,
  and the people had to drink it down.

Then opening the camp gate wide,
  Moses shouted, "Who is on God's side?"
All who repented of their sin
  showed their remorse by joining him.

Then they subdued all of the rest,
  who still insisted they knew best.
Their very names, both man and wife,
  God blotted from the *Book of Life*.

The Third Commandment (The Book of Job)

It's easy to misuse God's name.
  People take it frequently in vain.
If we're off guard, we might enter in,
  but the Bible says that it's a sin.

A man named Job always honored God's name
  and never said anything that would cause him shame.
God rewarded Job abundantly,
  With seven sons and daughters three.

God loved of Job's respect to tell,
  but Satan sneered, "You treat him well."
"Take back your gifts from this spoiled child,
  And you'll find he's not so sweet and mild."

So God let Satan put Job to the test,
  Removing the gifts with which he'd been blessed.
Raiders took his cattle and donkeys to keep,
  And a lightning fire burned up his sheep.

Robbers stole his camels and slaughtered his men.
  A storm destroyed his house with his children.
Boils covered his body as he lost his good health,
  and he sat grieving in ashes and filth.

Job fell to the ground and worshipped the Lord,
  exclaiming the following faithful words,
"I'll die with nothing, just as I came."
  "God gives and takes. Blessed be His name."

Job's wife could scarce believe her ears.
  "Curse God and die," she cried in tears.
Job said she was wrong even though she was sad.
  God had given them good; now they'd take the bad.

Job said, "I know that my Redeemer lives,
  and because He lives, I, too, shall live.
And when I've rotted in the grave,
  God will long for the creature His hand has made."

"In the last days, He'll stand upon the earth
  and raise me up in a second birth.
He'll argue my case before Himself,
  and put my sins up on a shelf."

Then God loved Job still even more
  and blessed him as He had before.
God granted Job prosperity
  and seven new sons and daughters three.

The Fourth Commandment
(Exodus 35:3 and Numbers 15:32-36)

God said in Commandment Number Four:
  "Work six days a week, not one day more.
Stick to your jobs quite loyally,
  but the seventh day is just for me."

"That's when you should lift up your praise,
  your presents bring, your voices raise.
You'll ask forgiveness for your sin
  and gather together once again."

This was not what everyone wished to do.
  The law put some people in a stew.
They cried, "This new law is a bore.
  We won't observe it anymore."

They saw no need they should relax.
  They were caught in deadlines, rules, and facts.
A holy day seemed a waste of time.
  To work was surely not a crime.

When the Hebrews fled from Egypt's land
  and wandered over the desert sand,
the Sabbath night could be cold and long
  for those whose firewood was gone.

One man caught in this very fault
  thought rules should be taken with a grain of salt.
He said, "I'm not so bad. I don't play tricks.
  So God shouldn't mind if I pick up sticks.

He said, "My firewood's gone; I need some more,"
  and then he walked outside his door.
He thought that he was in the right
  in gathering wood on a Sabbath night.

His neighbors watched. He could start a trend
  As he argued regarding God's laws for men,
"What's wrong if no one's getting hurt?
  It's too strict a reading of God's word."

But he was wrong as he could be.
  So he was taken in custody,
And the priests requested for God to say
  What to do with a man who dishonored His day.

God answered that the man must be
  punished there immediately.
Even for what seems a tiny straw,
  we must not disobey God's law.

The Fifth Commandment (Genesis 16, 21, and 22)

God's fifth command makes it apparent,
  we need to honor both our parents.
Submitting to our earthly sires
  shapes us to do what God desires.

This rule's more on the easy side
  if our parent's faith is deep and wide,
but becomes harder than it should
  if our parents' demands do not seem good.

Ishmael was Abraham's first-born boy.
  his birth brought his father tremendous joy,
but his father later, emotion-tossed,
  told Ishmael to go get lost.

Ishmael and his mother left in haste
  and wandered through the desert waste.
Run out of water, they thought they'd die,
  when God opened Ishmael's mother's eye.

She saw a well of water sweet
  that put them both back on their feet.
Ishmael obeyed his Dad without protest,
  and God saved him and left him blessed.

Isaac was Abraham's second boy.
  His birth, too, brought his father joy.
But his father later, his joy undone,
  agreed to sacrifice his son.

Leading a donkey with his hand,
  He set out across the desert sand.
Isaac came along behind.
  He showed his father he could mind.

But God then spoke his message loud:
  To hurt a child is not allowed.
God opened Isaac's father's eye.
  He saw a ram. Isaac didn't die.

God says, if we honor our parents' worth,
  That we'll live long upon the earth.
And these boys' descendants lived to be
  Great nations, a mighty progeny.

God showed he opposes hurting children.
  Parents can love their kids with discipline.
But can moderate spanks on the behind
  help teach a child that he should mind?

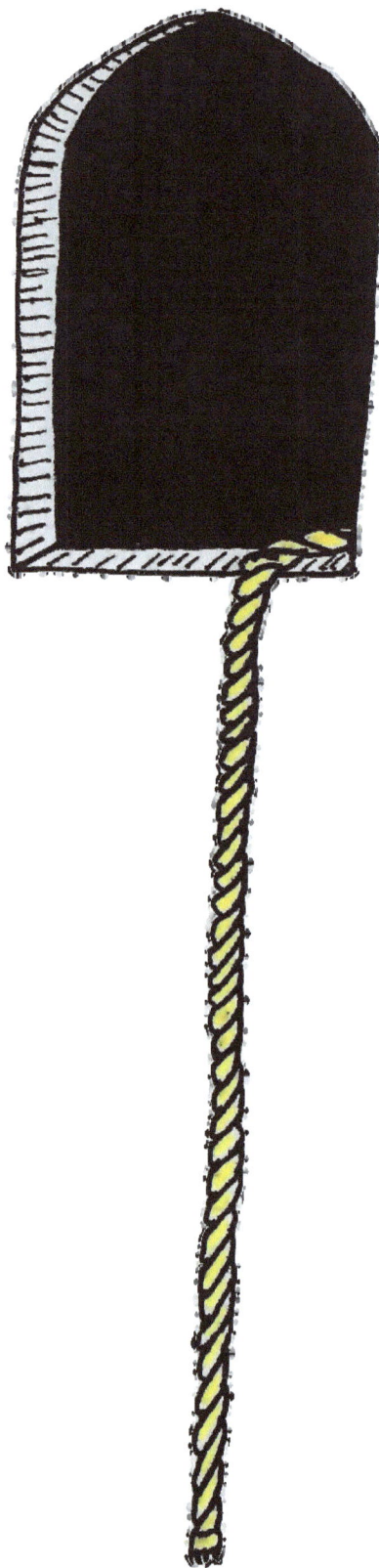

The Sixth Commandment
(I Samuel 19, 22, 24, 26, and 31)

Murder is a horrid crime,
  cutting short a person's given time.
Who knows what longer life had brought –
  a soul saved, a lesson taught.

When David was still just a young man,
  his praise was sung throughout the land.
When the giant Goliath caused fear and dread,
  David brought him down and cut off his head.

As leader of King Saul's army,
  David fought and beat the enemy.
His acts of valor quite amazed
  the people, who loudly sang his praise.

But King Saul was filled with jealousy,
  and treated David with hostility.
When David played the harp for him,
  Saul tried to spear him on his javelin.

Saul sent his guards to David's home
  to arrest him while he was alone.
But David saved himself by flight,
  climbing down a rope into the night.

While Saul behaved so murderously,
  David responded gallantly,
refusing to defy God's law
  by seeking revenge against King Saul.

When David hid in a cave at En-Gedi,
  Saul came in momentarily.
David in the dark came so close
  he cut a piece off of his robe.

On another occasion, David found
  Saul asleep upon the ground.
He took his water jug and spear,
  but spared his life and left him there.

King Saul, who showed such small belief,
  ended his life in shame and grief.
He met defeat and lost his land,
  and took his life with his own hand.

But David, who spared the life of Saul,
  ended up as master of it all.
After Saul had died, David became king
  and ruled over everything.

The Seventh Commandment (Genesis 39)

Disloyalty to spouse is serious;
  it follows murder on God's list.
For the Bible says that man and wife
  become as one, and that's for life.

To betray the other's trusting heart
  is to rip the very flesh apart.
And, if there are children, they are left
  of proper family bereft.

Joseph knew in advance what God decreed,
  and put it ahead of his own sad need.
Another who had lived such a difficult life
  might have thought it fair to play with somebody else's wife.

Joseph had been an outstanding lad.
  It seemed he would never face anything bad.
Wealthy, handsome, and talented,
  he was his father's favorite kid.

Then his world collapsed beneath his feet.
  He was thrown into a well of woes so deep
that he tumbled about as far as far as he could go:
  a slave in a foreign land, lowest of the low.

Yet even as a slave, Joseph's skills were so great,
  he soon was managing his master's whole estate.
But where he'd worn a colored coat so rare,
  he now wore just a loincloth, going around half bare.

Cut off from family and home,
  he had nothing left to call his own.
While his master prospered from Joseph's deeds,
  Nobody cared about Joseph's needs.

Then his master's wife reached out to him,
  forgetting her own kith and kin.
Despite being so fortunate and blessed,
  She wanted Joseph as the best.

But this was wrong, and Joseph told her so,
  and left her clutching a resounding "No!"
So Joseph lost the job he did so well,
  and landed in a prison cell.

But Joseph obeyed God, and in the end
  he became the Pharaoh's right-hand man.
And the priest of On's daughter, whom he'd saved from strife,
  became his own beloved wife.

The Eighth Commandment (Genesis 31, 32, and 35)

God tells us that we may not steal.
  Consider how the victims feel.
We may want something urgently,
  but, if we control ourselves, we act wisely.

God gives the flowers clothes so fair
  and guards the birds up in the air.
If we have faith, we need not think twice.
  Rachel lacked that faith and paid the price.

One of the toughest cases of 'what is mine'
  concerns inheritance in the family line.
When we grow up in our parents' home,
  we may think what's theirs is what we own.

Emotions quickly enter in,
  confusing possessions with esteem.
And when there's more than just one child,
  questions of fairness can drive you wild.

Rachel thought it was not so bad
  to take what she wanted from her dad.
Ever since she was still quite young,
  she'd loved the idols of gods in her parents' home.

So Rachel took the figures with her one day
  when she and her husband moved away.
It almost gave her dad a heart attack,
  and he tracked her down to get them back.

He searched all over throughout her home,
  but could not find where the statues had gone.
Rachel was anxiously watching him.
  Nobody guessed she was sitting on them.

"Excuse me for not getting up," she said.
  "I'm feeling sick and should be in bed."
At last, he father abandoned hope,
  but said, "I know you have them. I'm no dope."

This accusation made Rachel's husband mad
  because he didn't realize what she had.
He said, "You accuse us, but I don't know why.
  Let whoever stole your stupid figures die."

Rachel soon, her soul defiled,
  took to her bed to bear a child.
The baby lived, but Rachel died
  and was buried on the mountainside.

The Ninth Commandment (Acts 5:1-10)

"Liar, liar, pants on fire"
  is a label easy to acquire.
But why should we get so up tight
  over a little lie that is o so white?

A tiny pinch of prevarication
  can save hours and hours of explanation.
And people are so very gossipy;
  what they don't know will not hurt me.

Fibs lubricate imagination
  and help to spice up conversation.
Yet lies, though white as white can be,
  in this dirty world become muddy.

The smallest fib soon grows in size
  and weaves into a web of lies,
with jet black threads that leave a stain
  on all who enter their domain.

God prohibits any lie, though small,
  clearly saying, "Lie not at all."
We need to pay close heed to this.
  We break God's laws at our own risk.

There once was a man named Ananias,
  who asked his wife, "Who can deny us
if we sell our farm outside of town,
  but don't write our real profit down?"

His wife Sapphira exclaimed, "Lie, schmy!"
  What can it hurt? No one will die."
So they sold the land, and then they laid
  a part aside from what they made.

That Sunday they could hardly wait
  to place it in the collection plate,
saying it was all they had.
  The gift was good. The lie was bad.

They wanted to stand up in church
  and be applauded for their worth.
Though false, they wanted all to see
  their pretended generosity.

But God knew exactly what was what,
  and they fell dead upon the spot.
They were carried out the door.
  Money could not help them anymore.

The Tenth Commandment
(I Kings 21 and 22 and II Kings 9)

The last Commandment seems so small,
  some feel it should not be there at all.
It tells us not to feel envy,
  as it might do harm to somebody.

We may imprison desires round about,
  but bottled liquid can spill out,
and once it falls upon the floor,
  it quickly spreads out more and more.

Ruth was a woman whom, truth to tell,
  life had not treated very well.
She had good reason to feel envy,
  as was clear for all to see.

Her husband died and left her alone
  with almost nothing to call her own.
And her father-in-law, well, he died, too,
  which left her wondering what to do.

While other women might have fussed,
  their envy undermining trust,
Ruth tended her mother-in-law Naomi out in the cold,
  without son or husband, poor and old.

When Naomi returned to her former home,
  sad and broken and alone,
Ruth went along to care for her,
  treating her like her own mother.

When Naomi said, "You have a chance
  to turn back now and find romance,"
Ruth answered that her home would be
  in Naomi's land with her destiny.

Once there, Ruth humbly appealed
  for left-over wheat from a harvested field.
Watching happy families with plenty to eat,
  she remained joyful, thankful, and sweet.

But the Bible says those who in this life come last
  will be put first before their story's past.
Ruth caught a prosperous farmer's eye.
  He liked the fact she did not sigh.

She became the farmer's wife
  and gave Naomi a brand-new life.
God honored her with a family line
  That descended to Jesus over time.

Jesus and the Commandments
(Mark 12:28-34 and Matthew 22:35-40)

We find again, in the New Testament,
  Jesus summarized the Commandments
by telling us that we should find
  we love God with heart, and soul, and mind.

The Old Testament says with all your might,
  but Jesus reminds us in our fight,
more important than a muscle's strain,
  our greatest strength lies in our brain.

Jesus also told us that the way
  to show God our love from day to day
is to love each other, and he did give
  his life to show us how to live.

He had no place to lay his head.
  He didn't even have a bed.
He gave his life the world to save,
  to resurrect us from the grave.

Jesus gave us faith, and hope, and love.
  He brought salvation from above.
But the greatest gift that he bestowed
  was the overwhelming love he showed.

Conclusion (Numbers 15:38-41)

These are the ten rules to guide our lives,
  for sons and daughters, husbands, wives,
to which was added as the best
  to love our God and all the rest.

Beside ten fingers on our hands
  to help remember God's commands,
God told us to sew some ribbons blue
  through the fringes of our garments, too.

Our very clothes should plainly claim:
  We don't worship statues. We respect God's name.
We keep the Sabbath. We honor our parent's lives.
  We don't murder.
  We respect the bond between husbands and wives.
We refuse to steal or lie or have envy in our heart.
Since God so loved us, we will do our part.